SUCCESSFUL COOKING

SOUPS

INDEX

Contents

Soup Success

There's nothing quite like homemade soup. It's enjoyable and surprisingly easy to make if you follow a few commonsense rules, and can be dressed up or down to suit just about any occasion.

The French quotation states 'soup is to dinner what the gateway is to a building', meaning that the soup should be chosen carefully to lead the diners into the meal. With some soups, such as consommés and light broths, this is still the case, but many others have become delicious, nutritious, flavour-packed meals in their own right. Today there are many different types of soup, varying in preparation, creaminess and consistency. We have broths, chowders, bouillons, consommés, as well as all manner of creamy soups.

The story goes that the most famous soup of all, Minestrone, was first tasted during the Crusades when Italian soldiers boiled up meat in water to make a simple broth, then asked the neighbouring villagers to contribute vegetables and herbs. Such humble beginnings for one of the world's most popular dishes.

STOCK SECRETS

While soup is the ideal vehicle for using up odds and ends from the refrigerator, it is only as good as its ingredients, and the backbone of any good soup is its stock. There are several alternatives when choosing stock. You can use home-made, fresh or frozen stock available from some delicatessens or poultry shops, or tetra packs or cubes from the supermarket. The best stock will be home-made or fresh and, as it can be frozen, it is a good idea to cook up large quantities every time. Tetra packs are convenient, as are stock cubes; however, check the labels and choose cubes made from natural ingredients with no added MSG. Commercial stocks

SIMMERING SOUPS

Most recipes call for a heavy-based pan for making soup. This is so that the pan distributes heat evenly and prevents anything 'catching' on the bottom. A wide, shallow pan will allow too much evaporation. The recipe will state if the pan should be covered. If it is not to be covered the soup

will simmer and, as the liquid evaporates off it, it will reduce down and thicken. So, if your soup is still a little thin, simply simmer it uncovered for a while. Most soups are cooked at a gentle simmer, meaning that the surface of the soup is barely moving, while a simmer means the soup will be

moving faster but without bubbles breaking the surface. Boiling is when bubbles actively break the surface of the soup. Watch the soup and adjust the heat accordingly. If the recipe says to partially cover the pan, tilt the lid at an angle so that there is a gap for steam to escape.

The surface of a simmering soup moves quite quickly.

Bubbles will be breaking on the surface when the soup is boiling.

Tilt the lid at an angle if the recipe calls for a partially covered pan.

always tend to be much saltier than home-made, so taste the soup before seasoning with salt and pepper. Always season soup at the end of the cooking time, as long cooking concentrates the flavours.

Try to use the flavour stock called for in the recipe. A beef stock would be overpowering in a recipe that calls for chicken stock, although vegetarians might prefer to use vegetable stock in all their soups.

PUREEING AND STRAINING

Many soups are puréed before serving and there is a sensible way to go about this. Let the soup cool a little first, so that it is safe if it splashes. Cool it quickly by pouring it into a bowl, then wash the pan to take the puréed soup for reheating. Purée in either a food processor or a blender – a blender will give a finer result, though it tends to aerate the soup slightly. Always purée in batches, never filling the processor above halfway.

Occasionally, recipes ask for the soup to be strained, particularly if making the stock is part of the recipe. A fine sieve (not a colander) is usually adequate. Some clear soups need more than one straining, through a sieve lined with damp muslin. If you don't have muslin, use a clean damp chux (kitchen cloth).

AHEAD OF TIME

Many soups can be made in advance and do, in fact, benefit from overnight refrigeration as the flavours develop. Use commonsense to determine if any of the ingredients will not store well, for example if the soup has cream, add it when you are reheating for serving. The same goes for pasta; for instance, if you add the pasta to Minestrone, then leave it to sit around, it will be unpleasantly soggy. Generally, soups can be kept for up to 3 days in the refrigerator, or frozen in airtight containers or freezer bags for up to 1–3 months. A lot of soups become very thick on standing and need to be diluted when reheated. Use more of the same stock, water or cream, as appropriate. The seasoning will also need to be adjusted.

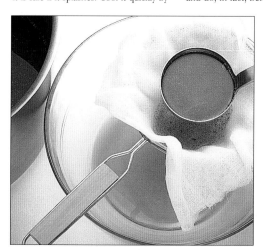

Clear soups can be strained through a sieve lined with damp muslin.

Some soups thicken on standing and need to be diluted when they are reheated.

Fennel, Asparagus and Pea Soup

PREPARATION TIME: 20 minutes
TOTAL COOKING TIME: 40 minutes
SERVES 4

30 g (1 oz) butter
1½ tablespoons olive oil
1 leek, white part only, sliced
1 fennel bulb, sliced
375 g (12 oz) asparagus, cut into pieces
1 clove garlic, crushed
8 mint leaves, chopped
150 g (5 oz) shelled or frozen peas
  (400 g/13 oz in pods)
200 g (6½ oz) potatoes, cubed
4 cups (1 litre) chicken or vegetable stock
pinch of cayenne pepper
pinch of ground nutmeg

Mint and garlic croutons
20 g (¾ oz) butter
1 tablespoon olive oil
2 slices day-old white bread, crusts removed,
  cut into four
mint leaves
2 cloves garlic, sliced, soaked in cold water

1 Heat the butter and oil in a large pan and add the leek and fennel. Cook over medium heat for 8–10 minutes, then stir in the asparagus, garlic, mint, peas and potato. Cook for 1 minute longer.

2 Add enough stock to cover the vegetables, and bring to the boil. Remove 4 asparagus tips, plunge into a bowl of iced water and set aside. Reduce the heat and simmer for 15–20 minutes, or until the vegetables are tender. Cool slightly then purée in a food processor. Return to the pan with the remaining stock, cayenne pepper and nutmeg and season.

3 Preheat the oven to moderately hot 190°C (375°F/Gas 5). To make the croutons, melt the butter and oil and brush on both sides of the bread. Lay on a baking tray. Tear the mint leaves in half, and place on the bread; dry the garlic and place on the mint. Drizzle the remaining butter mixture over the top. Bake for 5–6 minutes, or until the bread is toasted and the garlic golden.

4 Gently reheat the soup and serve garnished with the croutons and the reserved asparagus tips.

Split pods to remove peas; or string pod by pulling from top.

Using tongs, remove 4 asparagus tips and plunge into iced water.

Lay the mint leaves and garlic slices on the bread.

Cream of Tomato Soup

PREPARATION TIME: 25 minutes
TOTAL COOKING TIME: 30 minutes
SERVES 4

1.25 kg (2½ lb) tomatoes
1 tablespoon oil
1 onion, chopped
1 clove garlic, chopped
1½ cups (375 ml/12 fl oz) chicken stock
2 tablespoons tomato paste
1 teaspoon sugar
1 cup (250 ml/8 fl oz) cream

1 Cut a cross in the base of each tomato. Cover with boiling water for 1 minute, plunge in iced water, drain and peel away the skins. Scoop out the seeds and discard, then roughly chop the flesh.

2 Heat the oil in a large pan and cook the onion for 3 minutes, or until soft. Add the garlic and cook for 1 minute longer. Add the tomato and cook for 5 minutes, stirring occasionally, until very soft. Stir in the stock, bring to the boil, reduce the heat and simmer for 10 minutes.

3 Cool slightly, then transfer to a food processor. Process in batches until smooth, and return to the pan. Add the tomato paste and sugar and bring to the boil, stirring continuously. Reduce the heat and stir in the cream but do not allow the soup to boil. Season to taste before serving. Serve with an extra spoonful of cream and chopped parsley, if you want.

Plunge the tomatoes into iced water, then peel away the skin.

Cook, stirring with a wooden spoon, until tomato is very soft.

Add tomato paste and sugar and bring to the boil, stirring.

Lobster Bisque

PREPARATION TIME: 60 minutes
TOTAL COOKING TIME: 1 hour
SERVES 4

400 g (13 oz) raw lobster tail
100 g (3½ oz) butter, softened
7 spring onions, chopped
1 onion, chopped
1 carrot, chopped
4 cups (1 litre) fish stock
4 sprigs parsley
1 bay leaf
4 peppercorns
⅓ cup (40 g/1¼ oz) plain flour
1¾ cups (440 ml/14 fl oz) tomato purée
1 tablespoon sherry, optional
½ cup (125 ml/4 fl oz) cream
pinch of nutmeg
2 teaspoons chopped tarragon

1 Cut the lobster tail in half length-ways. Melt half the butter in a pan, add the spring onion and onion and cook for 5 minutes, or until soft but not coloured. Add the carrot and cook for 2 minutes. Add the lobster halves, fish stock, parsley, bay leaf, peppercorns and 2½ cups (600 ml/ 20 fl oz) of water. Bring to the boil, reduce the heat and simmer for 20 minutes, skimming the surface as required.

2 Remove the lobster from the stock, cool slightly and take the meat from the shells. Crush the shells and return to the pan. Continue simmering for a further 40 minutes. Strain the stock, then strain again through a sieve lined with 2 layers of damp muslin.

3 Cut some thin slices from the lobster to use as a garnish and set aside. In a blender, blend the remaining lobster flesh with a little of the strained stock until smooth. Mix the flour and remaining butter to a paste. Add the puréed lobster to the pan along with the flour paste, tomato purée, sherry, cream, nutmeg and salt and pepper, to taste. Mix well.

4 Add the tarragon and remaining stock and cook, stirring continuously, over high heat until the soup boils and thickens. Reduce the heat and simmer gently for 5 minutes. Season to taste and serve garnished with the reserved lobster and some sprigs of tarragon, if you want.

Lift meat out of lobster shells and lightly crush shells with a mallet.

Add puréed lobster, flour, tomato purée, sherry, cream and nutmeg.

Cream of Asparagus Soup

PREPARATION TIME: 20 minutes
TOTAL COOKING TIME: 55 minutes
SERVES 4–6

1 kg (2 lb) asparagus spears
30 g (1 oz) butter
1 onion, finely chopped
1 litre (4 cups) chicken stock
¼ cup (7 g/¼ oz) basil leaves, chopped
1 teaspoon celery salt
1 cup (250 ml/8 fl oz) cream

1 Break off woody ends from asparagus and trim off tips. Blanch the tips in boiling water for 1–2 minutes, refresh in cold water and set aside. Chop the remaining asparagus spears into large pieces.

2 Melt the butter in a large pan and cook the onion for 3–4 minutes over medium-low heat, or until soft and golden. Add the asparagus spears and cook for 1–2 minutes, stirring continuously.

3 Add chicken stock, basil and celery salt. Bring to the boil, reduce heat and simmer gently, covered, for 30 minutes.

4 Check that the asparagus is well cooked and soft. If not, simmer for a further 10 minutes. Set aside and allow to cool slightly.

5 Pour into a processor and process in batches until smooth. Sieve into a clean pan. Return to the heat, pour in cream and gently reheat. Do not allow the soup to boil. Season to taste with salt and pepper.

6 Serve immediately, with the asparagus tips placed on top of the soup.

Break off the woody ends from the asparagus spears.

Test whether asparagus is well cooked by piercing it with a fork.

Watercress and Potato Soup

PREPARATION TIME: 30 minutes
TOTAL COOKING TIME: 50 minutes
SERVES 6–8

30 g (1 oz) butter
2 onions, chopped
1–2 cloves garlic, chopped
1 kg (2 lb) potatoes, chopped into chunks
8 cups (2 litres) chicken stock
250 g (8 oz) watercress, trimmed
⅓ cup (80 ml/2¾ fl oz) cream

Parmesan croutons
2 slices bread, crusts removed
1 tablespoon olive oil
1 tablespoon grated Parmesan

1 Heat the butter in a large pan. Cook the onion and garlic for 2–3 minutes, or until softened. Add the potato and stir for 1–2 minutes. Add the stock and bring to the boil. Reduce the heat and simmer for 30 minutes, or until the potato is cooked. Strain, reserving the cooking liquid.

2 Transfer the potato mixture to a food processor, pour on about half the cooking liquid and process until smooth. Return to the pan.

3 In a food processor, process the watercress and 2 cups (500 ml/16 fl oz) of the cooking liquid until smooth. Pour the watercress mixture, cream and any remaining cooking liquid into the pan and combine. Stir over low heat for 3 minutes, or until warmed through, but do not allow the soup to boil. Season to taste.

4 To make the croutons, preheat the oven to moderate 180°C (350°F/Gas 4). Cut the bread into cubes and mix with the oil and grated Parmesan. Bake for 10 minutes, or until golden. Serve the croutons on top of the soup.

Pour in half the cooking liquid over the potato mixture.

Process watercress and liquid until smooth and pour into pan.

Quickly mix bread cubes in the oil and Parmesan until well coated.

Parsnip and Mustard Soup

PREPARATION TIME: 25 minutes
TOTAL COOKING TIME: 30 minutes
SERVES 4–6

30 g (1 oz) butter
1 onion, chopped
750 g (1½ lb) parsnips, chopped
4 cups (1 litre) chicken stock
½ cup (125 ml/4 fl oz) milk
½ cup (125 ml/4 fl oz) cream
2–3 tablespoons wholegrain mustard
2 tablespoons chopped flat-leaf parsley, to
  serve

1 Melt the butter in a large pan, add the onion and cook over moderate heat, stirring occasionally, until soft but not brown.

2 Add the parsnip and stock and bring to the boil. Simmer, covered, for 25 minutes, or until the parsnip is tender. Set aside to cool slightly.

3 Blend the soup in batches, in a blender or food processor. Return to the pan, add the milk and cream and reheat gently, but do not allow the soup to boil. Stir in the wholegrain mustard and season to taste with salt and freshly ground black pepper. Serve topped with the chopped parsley.

Cut peeled parsnips into strips, then chop into small pieces.

Add parsnip and chicken stock to the pan.

Using a wooden spoon, stir in the wholegrain mustard.

Vichyssoise

PREPARATION TIME: 10 minutes
TOTAL COOKING TIME: 45 minutes
SERVES 4–6

80 g (2¾ oz) butter
4 leeks, white part only, thinly sliced
1 white onion, thinly sliced
500 g (1 lb) potatoes, chopped
¼ teaspoon ground coriander
pinch of ground nutmeg
1 bay leaf
1 stick celery, quartered
3½ cups (875 ml/28 fl oz) chicken or
    vegetable stock
2 teaspoons lemon juice
½ cup (125 ml/4 fl oz) cream
chives, snipped, to garnish

1 Melt the butter in a large pan, add the leek and onion and fry gently, stirring occasionally, for 8–10 minutes, or until the vegetables are soft but not brown.

2 Add the potato, coriander, nutmeg, bay leaf, celery, stock and lemon juice. Bring to the boil, cover and simmer for 30 minutes, or until the vegetables are tender. Remove from the heat and allow to cool slightly. Remove the bay leaf and celery and discard.

3 Transfer to a food processor and process until smooth. Return to the pan. Whisk in the cream, then reheat gently without boiling. Serve either hot or cold, garnished with the chives.

Add the chopped potato to the vegetables in the pan.

Allow soup to cool a little before puréeing in batches until smooth.

Whisk in the cream and then reheat the soup without boiling.

Roasted Leek, Garlic and Bacon Soup

PREPARATION TIME: 25 minutes
TOTAL COOKING TIME: 1 hour 30 minutes
SERVES 4–6

1 tablespoon olive oil
20 g (¾ oz) butter
2 rashers bacon, chopped
3 leeks, chopped
2 cloves garlic, chopped
1 stick celery, coarsely chopped
2 zucchini, coarsely chopped
2 bay leaves
6 cups (1.5 litres) chicken stock
⅓ cup (80 ml/2¾ fl oz) cream
¼ cup (15 g/½ oz) finely chopped parsley
2 rashers bacon, extra, to serve

1 Preheat the oven to warm 160°C (315°F/Gas 2–3). Heat the oil and butter in a large roasting tin. Add the bacon rashers and stir over medium heat for 1–2 minutes. Add the leek, garlic, celery, zucchini and bay leaves and cook, stirring, for 2–3 minutes, without allowing to brown.

2 Transfer the roasting tin to the oven and roast the vegetables and bacon for 40 minutes, turning a couple of times. Cover with foil if starting to brown. Transfer to a large pan, pour on the stock and bring to the boil. Lower the heat and simmer for 30 minutes. Cool slightly, strain and return the liquid to the pan. Remove the bay leaves.

3 Put the vegetables and bacon in a food processor with a ladleful of the cooking liquid and process until smooth, adding more liquid if necessary. Return the purée to the pan with the liquid and add some pepper, the cream and parsley. Reheat gently.

4 To make the bacon garnish, trim off the rind and excess fat from the bacon and grill until crisp. Drain on paper towels, then crumble with your fingers and serve on top of the soup.

Turn vegetables while cooking and cover with foil.

Process vegetables and bacon until smooth.

Grill bacon until it is very crisp, then crumble to make a garnish.

Roasted Vegetable Soup

PREPARATION TIME: 30 minutes
TOTAL COOKING TIME: 1 hour 35 minutes
SERVES 6

2 carrots, cut into large pieces
1 parsnip, cut into large pieces
500 g (1 lb) unpeeled pumpkin, cut into
    large pieces
350 g (11 oz) unpeeled sweet potato, cut
    into large pieces
1 red capsicum, cut into large pieces
2 onions, halved
4 cloves garlic, unpeeled
3 cups (750 ml/24 fl oz) vegetable stock
sour cream and thyme, to serve

1 Preheat the oven to moderate 180°C (350°F/Gas 4). Put the vegetables in a large greased baking dish and brush lightly with some olive oil.

2 Bake for 1 hour, turning often. Remove the capsicum. Bake for 30 minutes longer; cool the vegetables slightly. Remove the skin from the capsicum; place in a food processor with the carrot, parsnip and onion.

3 Scrape the pumpkin and sweet potato flesh into the processor and squeeze in the garlic pulp. Add half the stock and purée until smooth. Place in a pan with the remaining stock and heat through. Season and serve with sour cream and thyme.

Cut carrots, parsnip, pumpkin and sweet potato into large pieces.

Using your fingers, peel away the blackened capsicum skin.

Using a teaspoon, scrape flesh from sweet potato and pumpkin.

Beef Consomme

PREPARATION TIME: 30 minutes
+ overnight refrigeration
TOTAL COOKING TIME: 5 hours
SERVES 4–6

1 kg (2 lb) gravy beef, cut into small pieces
500 g (1 lb) beef bones including marrow,
   cut into small pieces (ask your butcher to
   do this)
1 leek, cut into small pieces
2 onions, quartered
2 carrots, chopped
2 sticks celery, chopped
6 black peppercorns
6 whole cloves
3 sprigs thyme
3 sprigs parsley
3 bay leaves
1 egg shell, crumbled
1 egg white, lightly beaten
2 tablespoons chopped parsley

1 Preheat the oven to moderate
   180°C (350°F/Gas 4). Place the
gravy beef and beef bones in a single layer in a
baking dish. Bake for 45 minutes, or until lightly
browned, turning once.

2 Put the meat, bones, vegetables, peppercorns,
cloves, herbs, bay leaves and 1 teaspoon of salt in
a large pan. Add 3 litres of water and slowly bring
to the boil. Reduce the heat to low, cover and
simmer for 4 hours. Set aside to cool slightly.
Remove the larger pieces of meat and discard.
Ladle the liquid through a muslin-lined sieve into a
bowl. Discard the remaining meat and vegetables.

3 Cover the liquid and refrigerate for several hours,
or overnight. Spoon off the fat from the surface.
Return to a clean pan with the egg shell and the
lightly beaten egg white.

4 Slowly heat the stock to simmering and simmer
for 10 minutes. A frothy scum will form on the
surface. Remove from the heat and leave for
10 minutes. Skim the surface and ladle the stock
through a muslin-lined sieve. Reheat, season if
needed, and serve with the chopped parsley.

Lay gravy beef and bones in a single layer in a baking dish.

Carefully ladle stock into muslin-lined sieve placed over a bowl.

Gently stir in egg shell and egg white with a whisk.

Grilled Capsicum Soup with Herb Omelette

PREPARATION TIME: 20 minutes
TOTAL COOKING TIME: 50 minutes
SERVES 4–6

1 yellow or green capsicum, quartered
4 red capsicums, quartered
1 tablespoon olive oil
1 red onion, chopped
1 clove garlic, crushed
1 potato, diced
⅔ cup (170 ml/5½ fl oz) tomato juice
1 tablespoon balsamic vinegar

Herb omelette
3 eggs, lightly beaten
1 tablespoon milk
2 tablespoons chopped parsley
2 teaspoons oil
3 spring onions, finely chopped

1 Grill the capsicums skin-side-up under a hot grill until blackened. Place in a plastic bag and cool. Peel away the skin and dice the yellow and one of the red capsicums. Set aside the remaining red capsicum.

2 Heat the oil and cook the onion, stirring, over medium heat until transparent. Add the garlic and potato and cook, stirring, for 1 minute. Add the tomato juice and 3 cups (750 ml) water, bring to the boil, reduce the heat and cover. Simmer for 25 minutes, or until the potato is tender.

3 Blend the soup until smooth, in batches, with the reserved red capsicum. Return to the pan and add the diced capsicum, vinegar and seasoning. Reheat gently to serve.

4 To make the herb omelette, whisk the eggs, milk and parsley and season. Heat the oil in a frying pan. Add the spring onion and cook until just soft. Pour in the egg mixture and cook over moderate heat until set. Cool on a wire rack and cut into diamonds. Serve on top of the soup.

Dice the yellow capsicum and one of the red ones.

Add the reserved red capsicum to the blender or food processor.

It is best to use a non-stick frying pan, if you have one.

Roast Pumpkin Soup

PREPARATION TIME: 10 minutes

TOTAL COOKING TIME: 1 hour 45 minutes

SERVES 6

2 tablespoons olive oil
1 clove garlic, crushed
1½ teaspoons dried oregano
250 g (8 oz) Roma tomatoes, halved lengthways
850 g (1 lb 12 oz) butternut pumpkin,
  unpeeled, chopped
250 g (8 oz) carrots, quartered
180 g (6 oz) onions, quartered
200 g (6½ oz) sweet potato, chopped
1 tablespoon chopped oregano
6 cups (1.5 litres) chicken stock
flaked toasted almonds and oregano sprigs,
  to garnish

1 Preheat the oven to moderately hot 190°C (375°F/Gas 5). Mix the oil, garlic, oregano and ½ teaspoon of salt. Put the tomatoes, cut-side-up, in a roasting tin with the pumpkin, carrot, onion and sweet potato. Brush with the oil mixture and bake for 1½ hours. Cool. Scrape the flesh from the pumpkin and put in a large pan with the vegetables, oregano and stock.

2 Bring to the boil, reduce the heat and simmer for 10 minutes. Cool and purée in a blender or food processor. Reheat and season to taste. Garnish with the almonds and oregano sprigs.

Brush vegetables with oil mixture, leaving the tomatoes cut-side-up.

Scrape the flesh from the pumpkin using a teaspoon.

Purée the soup in batches in a blender or food processor.

Stock

SOUP IS A DISH WHOSE SUM IS DEFINITELY GREATER THAN ITS PARTS. AND ONE OF ITS MOST IMPORTANT PARTS IS STOCK. A GOOD STOCK MAKES THE DIFFERENCE BETWEEN AN ORDINARY AND A SPECTACULAR SOUP, GIVING FULL-BODIED FLAVOURS AND A SOUND BASE FOR THE OTHER INGREDIENTS. IF YOU ARE LOOKING AT THESE RECIPES AND THINKING THE COOKING TIMES SEEMING VERY LONG AND IT ALL LOOKS LIKE TOO MUCH TROUBLE, THINK AGAIN. IT DOESN'T TAKE LONG TO CHOP UP THE INGREDIENTS AND THEN YOU CAN LEAVE YOUR STOCK TO SIMMER LAZILY WHILE YOU GET ON WITH OTHER THINGS.

BEEF STOCK

PREPARATION TIME: 20 minutes
+ refrigeration
TOTAL COOKING TIME: 4 hours
50 minutes
MAKES about 7 cups (1.75 litres)

2 kg (4 lb) beef bones
2 unpeeled carrots, chopped
2 unpeeled onions, quartered
2 tablespoons tomato paste
2 sticks celery, leaves included, chopped
1 bouquet garni
12 black peppercorns

1 Preheat the oven to hot 210°C (415°F/Gas 6–7). Put the bones in a baking dish and bake for 30 minutes, turning occasionally. Add the carrot and onion and cook for a further 20 minutes. Allow to cool.

2 Put the bones, carrot and onion in a large, heavy-based pan. Drain the excess fat from the baking dish and pour 1 cup (250 ml/8 fl oz) of water into the dish. Stir to dissolve any juices; add the liquid to the pan.

3 Add the tomato paste, celery and 10 cups (2.5 litres) water. Bring to the boil, skimming the surface as required and add the bouquet garni and peppercorns. Reduce the heat to low and simmer gently for four hours. Skim the froth from the surface regularly.

4 Ladle the stock in batches into a fine sieve sitting over a bowl. Gently press the solids with a ladle to extract all the liquid. Discard the bones and vegetables and set aside to cool. Refrigerate until cold and spoon off any fat that has set on top. At this stage you can reduce the stock to concentrate its flavour (dilute before using) and store in the refrigerator for up to 2 days or in the freezer for up to 6 months.

FREEZING STOCKS

Freezing your stock is useful if you want to prepare ahead. Simply pour the stock into a measuring jug lined with a plastic bag to you can measure how much stock you have freeze it in convenient portions. Remove the bag from the jug, label the bag, seal securely and freeze.

Alternatively, pour the stock into ice cube trays and freeze. This is useful for fairly concentrated stocks.

CHICKEN STOCK

PREPARATION TIME: 20 minutes + refrigeration
TOTAL COOKING TIME: 3 hours 10 minutes
MAKES about 10 cups (2.5 litres)

2 kg (4 lb) chicken bones
2 unpeeled onions, quartered
2 unpeeled carrots, chopped
2 sticks celery, leaves included, chopped
1 bouquet garni
12 black peppercorns

1 Put the chicken bones, onion, carrot, celery and 14 cups (3.5 litres) of water in a large, heavy-based pan. Bring slowly to the boil. Skim the surface as required and add the bouquet garni and peppercorns. Reduce the heat to low and simmer gently for 3 hours. Skim the froth from the surface regularly.

2 Ladle the stock in batches into a fine sieve sitting over a bowl. Gently press the solids with a ladle to extract all the liquid. Let the stock cool, then refrigerate until cold and spoon off any fat that has set on the top. At this stage you can reduce the stock to concentrate its flavour (dilute before using) and store in the refrigerator for up to 2 days or in the freezer for up to 6 months.

FISH STOCK

PREPARATION TIME: 20 minutes
+ refrigeration
TOTAL COOKING TIME: 30 minutes
MAKES about 7 cups (1.75 litres)

2 kg (4 lb) chopped fish bones, heads
    and tails
1 stick celery, leaves included, roughly
    chopped
1 onion, chopped
1 unpeeled carrot, chopped
1 leek, sliced
1 bouquet garni
12 black peppercorns

1 Place the fish bones, celery, onion, carrot, leek and 8 cups (2 litres) water in a large, heavy-based pan. Bring slowly to the boil. Skim the surface as required and add the bouquet garni and peppercorns. Reduce the heat to low and simmer very gently for 20 minutes. Skim the froth from the surface regularly.

2 Ladle the stock in batches into a sieve line with damp muslin sitting over a bowl. To keep a clear fish stock, do not press the solids, but simply allow the stock to strain undisturbed. Allow to cool, then store in the refrigerator for up to 2 days or in the freezer for up to 6 months.

VEGETABLE STOCK

PREPARATION TIME: 20 minutes
+ refrigeration
TOTAL COOKING TIME: 1 hour
30 minutes
MAKES about 10 cups (2.5 litres)

1 tablespoon oil
1 onion, chopped
2 leeks, chopped
4 carrots, chopped
2 parsnips, chopped
4 sticks celery, leaves included, chopped
2 bay leaves
1 bouquet garni
4 unpeeled cloves garlic
8 black peppercorns

1 Heat the oil in a large, heavy-based pan and add the onion, leek, carrot, parsnip and celery. Cover and cook for 5 minutes without colouring. Add 12 cups (3 litres) of water. Bring to the boil. Skim the surface if required, and add the bay leaves, bouquet garni, garlic and peppercorns. Reduce the heat to low and simmer for 1 hour. Skim the froth from the surface of the stock regularly.

2 Ladle the stock in batches into a fine sieve sitting over a bowl. Gently press the solids to extract all the liquid.

3 Allow the stock to cool, then refrigerate until cold and spoon off any fat that has set on the top. At this stage you can reduce the stock to concentrate its flavour (dilute before using) and store in the refrigerate for up to 2 days or in the freezer for up to 6 months.

Note: Like a bouquet garni, unpeeled garlic added to a stock adds a subtle flavour that will not cloud the soup.

BOUQUET GARNI

To make a bouquet garni, wrap the green part of a leek loosely around a bay leaf, sprig of thyme, some celery leaves and a few stalks of parsley, then tie with string. Leave enough string for easy removal.

Moroccan Chickpea Soup

PREPARATION TIME: 35 minutes
+ overnight soaking
TOTAL COOKING TIME: 1 hour 10 minutes
SERVES 4

250 g (8 oz) dried chickpeas
2 tablespoons olive oil
1 onion, finely sliced
2 teaspoons ground cumin
2 teaspoons sweet paprika
1 teaspoon ground ginger
1 teaspoon ground cinnamon
¼ teaspoon allspice
250 g (8 oz) boneless lamb leg steaks, cut
  into strips
500 g (1 lb) tomatoes, finely chopped
8 cups (2 litres) vegetable stock or water
2 teaspoons grated lemon rind
½ cup (110 g/3½ oz) short-grain rice
¼ cup (7 g/¼ oz) chopped parsley
2 tablespoons chopped coriander

1 Soak the chickpeas in cold water overnight. Drain. Heat the oil in a large pan over low heat and add the onion and spices. Cook for 15 minutes, covered, stirring occasionally.

2 Add the chickpeas, lamb, tomato and stock. Bring to the boil, reduce the heat and simmer for 35 minutes. Skim the surface as required. Add the lemon rind and rice and cook for 12 minutes, or until the rice is tender. Add the herbs and season to taste.

Soak chickpeas in cold water and leave overnight. Drain well.

Use a sharp knife to cut the lamb leg steaks into strips.

Add onion, cumin, paprika, ginger, cinnamon and allspice to the pan.

Saffron Fish Soup

PREPARATION TIME: 20 minutes
TOTAL COOKING TIME: 30 minutes
SERVES 4

1 kg (2 lb) white fish bones (heads and
  trimmings), chopped
2 cups (500 ml/16 fl oz) dry white wine
1 onion, chopped
1 carrot, chopped
1 stick celery, chopped
1 bay leaf
6 black peppercorns
¾ teaspoon saffron threads
50 g (1¾ oz) butter
¼ cup (30 g/1 oz) plain flour
12 scallops, trimmed
250 g (8 oz) boneless white fish fillets, cut
  into cubes
1 cup (250 ml/8 fl oz) cream

1 To make the saffron fish stock, place the fish
bones, 3 cups (750 ml/24 fl oz) of water, the
wine, onion, carrot, celery, bay leaf and peppercorns in a large pan. Bring to the boil slowly,
skimming the surface as required. Simmer,
covered, for 20 minutes. Strain and discard the
fish and vegetables. Take 4 cups (1 litre) of the hot
stock and stir in the saffron threads. (If you have
any stock leftover at this stage, you can simply
freeze it for use in another recipe.)

2 Melt the butter in a large pan and stir in the flour.
Cook, stirring continuously, over low heat for
3 minutes but do not allow the mixture to colour.
Remove from the heat and gradually pour in the
reserved fish stock. Return to the heat and stir
continuously until the mixture boils and thickens
slightly. Add the scallops and fish cubes, bring
back to the boil and simmer for 1–2 minutes.

3 Stir in the cream and reheat gently, but do not
allow the soup to boil. Season to taste with salt
and freshly ground white pepper. Garnish with
sprigs of chervil, if you want.

*Using a sharp knife, remove the
dark vein from the scallops.*

*Combine reserved hot fish stock
and saffron threads in a jug.*

*Add scallops and fish cubes to the
soup and simmer for 1–2 minutes.*

Potato and Cheese Soup

PREPARATION TIME: 20 minutes
TOTAL COOKING TIME: 40 minutes
SERVES 4–6

30 g (1 oz) butter
4 rashers bacon, cut into strips
1 onion, finely chopped
½ teaspoon sweet paprika
1 kg (2 lb) potatoes, chopped
3 cups (750 ml/24 fl oz) chicken stock
1 cup (125 g/4 oz) grated Cheddar
chopped chives, to serve

1 Melt the butter in a large pan, add the bacon and cook until crisp. Remove the bacon from the pan with a slotted spoon, leaving as much fat as possible. Add the onion to the same pan and cook for 5 minutes, or until very soft and golden. Add the paprika and cook for a further 30 seconds.

2 Return the bacon to the pan and add the potato and stock. Bring to the boil, then reduce the heat and simmer for 30 minutes, or until the potato is very soft. Stir or mash lightly to break up the potato. Add the Cheddar and stir well, until it is melted through. Season with salt and pepper to taste and serve topped with a sprinkling of chopped chives.

Trim the rind and excess fat from the bacon and cut into strips.

Cook bacon until crisp and remove from pan with a slotted spoon.

Stir with a wooden spoon or mash lightly to break up potato.

Bouillabaisse

PREPARATION TIME: 40 minutes
TOTAL COOKING TIME: 1 hour 20 minutes
SERVES 4–6

4–6 tomatoes
500 g (1 lb) raw king prawns
1 raw lobster tail
1–2 fish heads
1 cup (250 ml/8 fl oz) red wine
3 onions, finely chopped
6 cloves garlic, crushed
3 bay leaves
¼ cup (60 ml/2 fl oz) olive oil
1 leek, finely sliced
¼ cup (60 g/2 oz) tomato paste
small piece of orange rind
500 g (1 lb) white fish fillet, cut into small
   pieces
12 mussels, firmly closed, scrubbed and
   beards removed
200 g (6½ oz) scallops with corals
½ cup (30 g/1 oz) chopped parsley
¼ cup (15 g/½ oz) shredded basil leaves

1 Score a cross in the base of each tomato. Cover with boiling water for 1 minute, plunge in cold water, drain and peel away the skins.

2 To make the fish stock, peel and devein prawns and set shells, heads and tails aside. Shell lobster tail, keeping shell and chopping meat. Put lobster shell, fish heads, prawn shells, heads and tails in a large pan. Add wine, 1 onion, 2 cloves garlic, 1 bay leaf and 2 cups (500 ml/16 fl oz) of water. Bring to the boil, reduce heat and simmer for 20 minutes. Strain through a fine sieve, reserving stock.

3 Heat oil in a large, heavy-based pan. Add leek and remaining onion and garlic. Cover and simmer, stirring occasionally, over low heat for 20 minutes, or until browned. Add the tomato, remaining bay leaves, tomato paste and orange rind and stir well. Remove lid and continue to cook for 10 minutes, stirring occasionally. Add the reserved fish stock, bring to the boil, reduce the heat and simmer for 10 minutes, stirring occasionally.

4 Add prawns, lobster, fish pieces, mussels and scallops. Simmer, covered, for 4–5 minutes. Discard any unopened mussels, the rind and bay leaves. Add the herbs and season to taste with salt and freshly ground black pepper. The Bouillabaisse is shown here with a bowlful of Rouille, a delicious accompaniment.

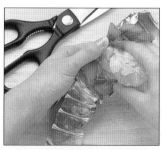

Cut on either side of soft underside of lobster tail, and lift up.

Strain through a fine sieve, reserving the stock.

French Onion Soup

PREPARATION TIME: 15 minutes
TOTAL COOKING TIME: 1 hour 30 minutes
SERVES 4–6

1 tablespoon olive oil
30 g (1 oz) butter
1 kg (2 lb) onions, thinly sliced
1½ tablespoons soft brown sugar
4 tablespoons plain flour
6 cups (1.5 litres) beef stock
½ cup (125 ml/4 fl oz) brandy
¼ cup (60 ml/2 fl oz) olive oil, extra
2 cloves garlic, crushed
1 French bread stick
1 cup (100 g/3½ oz) grated Parmesan

1 Heat the oil and butter in a large, heavy-based pan. Add the onion and stir over low heat for 1 minute. Cover and cook for a further 20 minutes, stirring occasionally. Add the sugar and ½ teaspoon of salt and increase the heat. Cook for 30 minutes, stirring frequently, or until the onion is golden brown.

2 Gradually add the flour. Cook for 3 minutes over medium heat, stirring. Remove from the heat and gradually add the combined stock and brandy.

3 Over medium heat, bring to the boil, stirring constantly, until slightly thickened. Partially cover the sauce-pan, lower the heat and simmer gently for 30 minutes, stirring occasionally. Season to taste.

4 Mix the extra oil and garlic. Cut the bread stick into thick slices and toast both sides under a preheated grill, until lightly browned. Brush on the oil and sprinkle with the Parmesan. Grill until melted and serve on the soup.

Cook onion, stirring frequently, until it is a rich golden brown.

Gradually add combined stock and brandy.

Using a pastry brush, coat one side of the toast with oil mixture.

Cuban Black Bean Soup

PREPARATION TIME: 20 minutes
+ overnight soaking
TOTAL COOKING TIME: 1 hour 40 minutes
SERVES 6

2 cups (440 g/14 oz) dried black beans
2 tablespoons oil
1 onion, sliced
2 teaspoons ground cumin
1 teaspoon ground coriander
½ teaspoon chilli powder
2 cloves garlic, crushed
300 g (10 oz) bacon bones
2 tablespoons red wine vinegar
1 tablespoon soft brown sugar
3 spring onions, chopped
1 tablespoon chopped parsley
2 hard-boiled eggs, chopped

1 Soak the black beans in plenty of cold water overnight. Drain.

2 Heat the oil in a large, heavy-based pan and cook the onion over medium heat for 5 minutes, or until softened. Add the cumin, coriander, chilli powder and garlic to the pan and cook for 1 minute.

3 Add the bacon bones and 5 cups (1.2 litres) of water, stirring well. Add the beans and bring to the boil; reduce the heat and simmer, partially covered, for 1–1½ hours, or until the beans are very soft.

4 Using a pair of tongs, remove the bacon bones from the pan and discard. Stir in the vinegar and sugar and season to taste. If you want a thicker soup, mash the beans slightly with a potato masher. Garnish with the spring onion, parsley and hard-boiled egg.

Add all the spices and crush the garlic into the pan.

The beans should be soft when crushed with a fork.

Remove the bacon bones from the pan with a pair of tongs.

Won Ton Soup

PREPARATION TIME: 50 minutes
+ 30 minutes soaking
TOTAL COOKING TIME: 40 minutes
SERVES 4

2 dried Chinese mushrooms
15 raw prawns
100 g (3½ oz) pork mince
2 spring onions, chopped
1 teaspoon grated ginger
2 tablespoons canned water chestnuts,
   chopped
2 teaspoons chopped lemon grass, white
   part only
1 clove garlic, finely chopped
3 tablespoons soy sauce
225 g (7 oz) won ton wrappers
coriander leaves
6 cups (1.5 litres) beef stock
3 baby carrots, cut diagonally
3 spring onions, cut diagonally

1 Soak the mushrooms in hot water for 30 minutes. Peel and devein the prawns, then cut in half lengthways. Drain the mushrooms, remove the stems and chop the caps.

2 Mix the chopped mushroom with the pork, spring onion, ginger, water chestnut, lemon grass, garlic and 1 tablespoon of the soy sauce. Work with 1 won ton wrapper at a time, keeping the rest covered. Put 2–3 coriander leaves, half a prawn and a heaped teaspoon of the pork mixture in the centre of a wrapper. Brush the edges with water and lay another wrapper on top. Press to seal. Repeat with the remaining wrappers.

3 Bring the stock, remaining soy sauce, carrot and spring onion to the boil. Bring another large pan of water to the boil and cook the won tons in batches for 4–5 minutes; drain. Pour the hot soup over the won tons.

Thinly slice the white part of the lemon grass, then chop finely.

Remove stems from soaked mushrooms and finely chop the caps.

Lightly brush edges with water, then lay another wrapper on top.

Chickpea, Chorizo and Pork Rib Soup

PREPARATION TIME: 20 minutes
+ overnight soaking
TOTAL COOKING TIME: 40 minutes
SERVES 6–8

180 g (6 oz) dried chickpeas
300 g (10 oz) smoked bacon ribs
2 tablespoons olive oil
1 onion, finely chopped
1 clove garlic, crushed
2 tomatoes, peeled, seeded and finely
  chopped
1 potato, cubed
1 carrot, sliced
200 g (6½ oz) pumpkin, chopped
150 g (5 oz) chorizo or pepperoni sausage,
  sliced
¼ teaspoon dried oregano
6 cups (1.5 litres) chicken stock

1 Soak the chickpeas in cold water overnight. Drain.

2 Blanch bacon ribs in boiling water for 30 seconds, then plunge into iced water. Drain and slice into pieces.

3 Heat the oil in a large, heavy-based pan and cook the onion over medium heat for 3–4 minutes, stirring continuously. Add the garlic and tomato and cook for a further 5 minutes.

4 Add the chickpeas, ribs, potato, carrot, pumpkin, chorizo, dried oregano and stock. Bring to the boil, then reduce the heat and simmer, covered, for 30 minutes, or until the chickpeas are tender. Season to taste.

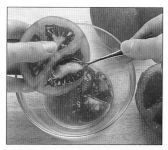

Halve peeled tomatoes and scoop out the seeds using a teaspoon.

Use chorizo, pepperoni or another type of spicy sausage.

Drain the blanched ribs, then cut into smaller sections.

49

Thai-Style Chicken and Baby Corn Soup

PREPARATION TIME: 30 minutes
TOTAL COOKING TIME: 15 minutes
SERVES 4

150 g (5 oz) whole baby corn
1 tablespoon oil
2 stalks lemon grass, white part only, very finely sliced
2 tablespoons finely grated ginger
6 spring onions, chopped
1 red chilli, finely chopped
4 cups (1 litre) chicken stock
1½ cups (375 ml/12 fl oz) coconut milk
250 g (8 oz) chicken breast fillets, thinly sliced
130 g (4¼ oz) creamed corn
1 tablespoon soy sauce
2 tablespoons finely chopped chives, to serve
1 red chilli, thinly sliced, to serve

1 Cut the baby corn in half or quarters lengthways, depending on their size. Set aside.

2 Heat the oil in a pan over medium heat and cook the lemon grass, ginger, spring onion and chilli for 1 minute, stirring continuously. Add the stock and coconut milk and bring to the boil—do not cover or the coconut milk will curdle.

3 Stir in the corn, chicken and creamed corn and simmer for 8 minutes, or until the corn and chicken are just tender. Add the soy sauce, season well and serve garnished with the chives and chilli.

Grate the peeled ginger on the fine side of the grater.

Cut the baby corn lengthways into halves or quarters.

Add the corn, chicken and creamed corn to the pan.

Gazpacho

PREPARATION TIME: 40 minutes
+ 3 hours refrigeration
TOTAL COOKING TIME: Nil
SERVES 4–6

750 g (1½ lb) ripe tomatoes
1 Lebanese cucumber, chopped
1 green capsicum, chopped
2–3 cloves garlic, crushed
1–2 tablespoons finely chopped black olives
(optional)
⅓ cup (80 ml/2¾ fl oz) red or white wine
vinegar
¼ cup (60 ml/2 fl oz) olive oil
1 tablespoon tomato paste

Accompaniments
1 onion, finely chopped
1 red capsicum, finely chopped
2 spring onions, finely chopped
1 Lebanese cucumber, finely chopped
2 hard-boiled eggs, chopped
chopped mint or parsley
Garlic and herb croutons

1 Score a cross in the base of each tomato. Cover with boiling water for 1 minute, plunge into cold water, drain and peel away the skins. Chop the flesh so finely that it is almost a purée.

2 Mix together the tomato, cucumber, capsicum, garlic, olives, vinegar, oil, and tomato paste, and season to taste. Cover and refrigerate for 2–3 hours.

3 Use 2–3 cups (750 ml/24 fl oz) of chilled water to thin the soup to your taste. Serve chilled, with the chopped onion, capsicum, spring onion, cucumber, boiled egg, herbs and croutons served separately for diners to add to their own bowls.

Halve the cucumber lengthways, cut into strips and chop finely.

Put tomatoes in a heatproof bowl and cover with boiling water.

Using a sharp knife, chop tomato flesh very finely to a purée.

Smoked Haddock Chowder

PREPARATION TIME: 20 minutes
TOTAL COOKING TIME: 35 minutes
SERVES 4–6

500 g (1 lb) smoked haddock
1 potato, diced
1 stick celery, diced
1 onion, finely chopped
50 g (1¾ oz) butter
1 rasher bacon, rind removed and finely
  chopped
2 tablespoons plain flour
½ teaspoon dried mustard
½ teaspoon Worcestershire sauce
1 cup (250 ml/8 fl oz) milk
½ cup (15 g/½ oz) chopped parsley
¼ cup (60 ml/2 fl oz) cream (optional)

1 To make the fish stock, put the fish in a frying pan, cover with water and bring to the boil. Reduce the heat and simmer for 8 minutes, or until the fish flakes easily. Drain, reserving the fish stock, then peel, bone and flake the fish. Set aside.

2 Put the potato, celery and onion in a medium pan and pour over enough reserved fish stock to cover the vegetables. Bring to the boil, reduce the heat and simmer for 8 minutes, or until the vegetables are tender. Set aside.

3 Melt the butter in a large pan, add the bacon and cook, stirring, for 3 minutes. Add the flour, mustard and Worcestershire sauce and stir until combined. Cook for 1 minute. Remove from the heat and gradually pour in the milk, stirring continuously, until smooth. Return to the heat and stir for 5 minutes, until the mixture comes to the boil and has thickened. Stir in the vegetables and remaining stock, then add the parsley and fish. Simmer over low heat for 5 minutes, or until heated through. Taste for seasoning and serve with some cream, if you want.

Simmer haddock in a pan until it flakes when lifted with a fork.

Lay fish on paper towels to drain well, then flake into small pieces.

Gradually add milk, stirring with a wooden spoon.

Pea and Ham Soup

PREPARATION TIME: 20 minutes
TOTAL COOKING TIME: 2 hours 45 minutes
SERVES 6–8

1 tablespoon oil
2 onions, diced
2 carrots, diced
2 sticks celery, diced
1 parsnip, diced
1½ cups (330 g/10½ oz) green split peas
1 teaspoon black peppercorns
2 teaspoons dried thyme leaves
1 ham hock (850 g/1 lb 12 oz), cut into
  smaller pieces (ask your butcher to do this)

1 Heat the oil in a large pan and add the onion, carrot, celery and parsnip. Cook over low heat for 10 minutes, or until the vegetables have softened and the onion is translucent.

2 Add the split peas, peppercorns, thyme, the pieces of ham hock and 8 cups (2 litres) of water. Slowly bring to the boil, reduce the heat to low and simmer, covered, for 2½ hours, or until most of the meat has fallen off the bones and the vegetables and split peas are very soft. Stir occasionally.

3 Remove the bones from the pan, pulling off any of the meat that hasn't fallen away. Chop any large pieces and return to the pan. Season well with salt and pepper, if necessary.

Using a sharp knife, dice onions, carrots, celery and parsnip.

Add pieces of ham hock to the softened vegetables in the pan.

Trim off any meat that hasn't fallen away from the bones.

Scotch Broth

PREPARATION TIME: 40 minutes
+ 1 hour soaking + overnight refrigeration
TOTAL COOKING TIME: 4 hours
SERVES 8

1 kg (2 lb) lamb shanks, cut in half through
   the bone (ask your butcher to do this)
3 onions, chopped
3 turnips, chopped
2 carrots, chopped
1 tablespoon black peppercorns
½ cup (110 g/3½ oz) pearl barley
1 carrot, diced, extra
2 onions, finely chopped, extra
1 leek, chopped
1 stick celery, diced
2 turnips, diced, extra
chopped flat-leaf parsley

1 To make the stock, put the lamb shanks, onion, turnip, carrot, pepper-corns and 8 cups (2 litres) of water in a large pan. Bring to the boil, reduce the heat and simmer, covered, for 3 hours. Skim the surface as required.

2 Remove the shanks and any meat that has fallen off the bones and cool slightly. Remove the meat from the bones and finely chop, then cover and refrigerate. Strain the stock, discarding the vegetables. Cool the stock and refrigerate overnight, or until the fat has set on top and can be spooned off. Cover the barley with water and soak for 1 hour.

3 Put the stock in a large pan and gently reheat. Add the drained barley, extra carrot, onion, leek, celery and turnip. Bring to the boil, reduce the heat and simmer for 30 minutes, or until the barley and vegetables are just cooked. Return the meat to the pan and simmer for 5 minutes. Season well and serve with the parsley.

Use a skimmer or slotted spoon to skim the surface of the stock.

Place the barley in a bowl and cover with plenty of cold water.

The vegetables for the soup should be evenly and finely diced.

Mulligatawny Soup

PREPARATION TIME: 25 minutes
TOTAL COOKING TIME: 1 hour 25 minutes
SERVES 4–6

500 g (1lb) chicken thigh fillets, excess fat
   removed
2 tablespoons plain flour
1 tablespoon curry powder
1 teaspoon ground turmeric
30 g (1 oz butter)
1 onion, finely chopped
1 apple, peeled cored and finely chopped
4 cups (1 litre) chicken stock
6 whole cloves
⅓ cup (64 g/2¼ oz) basmati rice
1 tablespoon lemon juice
¼ cup (60 ml/2 fl oz) cream

1 Coat the chicken in the combined plain flour, curry powder and turmeric. Heat half the butter in a large pan and cook the chicken over medium heat for 3–4 minutes, or until lightly browned; turn frequently. Remove from the pan and drain on paper towels.

2 Add the remaining butter to the pan, then add the onion, apple and remaining flour mixture and cook for 3 minutes, or until soft. Return the chicken to the pan along with the stock and cloves. Bring to the boil, reduce the heat and simmer, covered, for 1 hour. Add the rice during the last 15 minutes and cook until it is tender.

3 Remove the chicken; allow to cool slightly and chop finely. Remove the cloves and skim any oil from the surface. Return the chicken to the pan. Reheat gently, stir in the lemon juice and cream, but do not allow the soup to boil. Season to taste with salt and freshly ground black pepper.

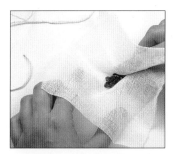

Cut out a square of muslin and tie up the cloves to make a pouch.

Mix flour and spices and toss in the chicken to coat.

Add rice to the simmering soup for the last 15 minutes of cooking.

Tom Kha Gai

PREPARATION TIME: 20 minutes
TOTAL COOKING TIME: 20 minutes
SERVES 4

5 cm (2 inch) piece of fresh galangal or
  5 slices of dried galangal
6 kaffir lime leaves
1 stem lemon grass, white part only,
  quartered
2 cups (500 ml/16 fl oz) coconut milk
2 cups (500 ml/16 fl oz) chicken stock
3 chicken breast fillets, cut into thin strips
1–2 teaspoons finely chopped red chillies
¼ cup (60 ml/2 fl oz) lime juice
2 tablespoons fish sauce
1 teaspoon soft brown sugar
¼ cup (15 g/½ oz) coriander leaves

1 Peel the galangal and cut into thin slices. Mix the galangal, kaffir lime leaves and lemon grass with the coconut milk and stock in a medium pan. Bring to the boil, reduce the heat to low and simmer for 10 minutes, stirring occasionally.

2 Add the chicken strips and chilli and simmer for 8 minutes. Mix in the lime juice, fish sauce and sugar. Serve with the coriander leaves and garnish with coriander sprigs, if you want.

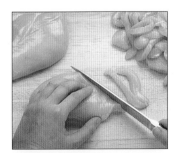

Using a sharp knife, cut chicken breast fillets into thin strips.

Using a vegetable peeler, peel the fresh galangal and slice thinly.

Add the soft brown sugar to the soup and stir to dissolve.

Roasted Tomato Soup

PREPARATION TIME: 20 minutes
TOTAL COOKING TIME: 1 hour 10 minutes
SERVES 4

1 kg (2 lb) Roma tomatoes
5 cloves garlic, unpeeled
5 tablespoons olive oil
1 teaspoon dried basil
3 tablespoons olive oil, extra
1 onion, finely chopped
1 red chilli, finely chopped
2 tablespoons balsamic vinegar
2 teaspoons soft brown sugar
1 tablespoon plain flour
4 cups (1 litre) vegetable stock
¼ cup (7 g/¼ oz) chopped flat-leaf parsley, to
 serve

1 Preheat the oven to moderately hot 200°C (400°F/ Gas 6). Halve tomatoes and lay cut-side-up in a baking tray with the garlic. Add the oil, some seasoning and the basil. Roast for 30 minutes. Take the garlic out after 20 minutes if it is drying out.

2 Heat the extra oil in a heavy-based pan. Add the onion and chilli and cook, covered, for 10 minutes over medium heat, stirring frequently.

3 Chop the tomatoes and squeeze the garlic pulp from their skins. Add to the pan along with the vinegar and sugar. Cook, stirring, for 1 minute. Stir in the flour and cook for 30 seconds.

4 Remove from the heat and add the stock. Return to the heat and bring to the boil, stirring occasionally. Simmer for 5 minutes. Season to taste and add the parsley.

Sprinkle basil over halved tomatoes and unpeeled garlic cloves.

Squeeze the garlic pulp from their skins and add to the pan.

Add the chopped flat-leaf parsley to the soup just before serving.

Rustic Hot Pot

PREPARATION TIME: 40 minutes
+ 1 hour refrigeration
TOTAL COOKING TIME: 2 hours
SERVES 4

2 tablespoons olive oil
8 lamb shanks
2 onions, sliced
4 cloves garlic, finely chopped
3 bay leaves, torn in half
1–2 teaspoons hot paprika
2 teaspoons sweet paprika
1 tablespoon plain flour
3 tablespoons tomato paste
6 cups (1.5 litres) vegetable stock
4 potatoes, chopped
4 carrots, sliced
3 sticks celery, thickly sliced
3 tomatoes, seeded and chopped

1 To make lamb stock, heat 1 tablespoon of the oil in a large, heavy-based pan over medium heat. Brown the shanks well in two batches and drain on paper towels.

2 Add remaining tablespoon of oil to pan and cook onion, garlic and bay leaves over low heat for 10 minutes, stirring regularly. Add paprikas and flour and cook, stirring, for 2 minutes. Gradually add combined tomato paste and stock. Bring to the boil, stirring, and return shanks to the pan. Reduce heat to low and simmer, covered, for 1½ hours, stirring occasionally.

3 Remove bay leaves and discard. Remove shanks, allow to cool slightly and then cut the meat from the bone. Discard bones. Cut meat into pieces and refrigerate. Refrigerate stock for about 1 hour, or until fat forms on surface and can be spooned off.

4 Return the meat to the soup along with the potato, carrot and celery and bring to the boil. Reduce the heat and simmer for 15 minutes. Season and add the chopped tomato to serve.

Brown shanks in 2 batches, remove with tongs and drain.

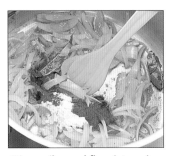
Stir paprikas and flour into onion mixture until it begins to colour.

Spoon off the fat that forms on the surface of the soup.

Spring Vegetable Soup

PREPARATION TIME: 30 minutes
+ overnight soaking
TOTAL COOKING TIME: 1 hour 15 minutes
SERVES 8

½ cup (105 g/3½ oz) pinto beans
2 teaspoons olive oil
2 onions, finely chopped
2 cloves garlic, finely chopped
10 cups (2.5 litres) vegetable stock
2 sticks celery, finely chopped
2 carrots
2 potatoes
150 g (5 oz) green beans
2 zucchini
100 g (3½ oz) shelled peas
2 tablespoons chopped flat-leaf parsley

1 Soak the pinto beans in plenty of cold water overnight. Drain.

2 Heat the oil in a large pan, add the onion and cook over low heat until soft and translucent. Add the garlic and cook for 1 minute further. Add the pinto beans, stock and celery and bring to the boil. Reduce the heat to low and simmer, covered, for 45 minutes, or until the beans are almost cooked.

3 Finely chop the carrots, potatoes, green beans and zucchini and add to the pan. Simmer gently for 15 minutes, or until the vegetables are almost cooked. Stir in the peas and simmer for a further 10 minutes.

4 Season well and stir through the chopped parsley.

Add drained pinto beans to pan and stir in with a wooden spoon.

Chop all the vegetables into small, even-sized dice.

Hot Beef Borscht

PREPARATION TIME: 30 minutes
TOTAL COOKING TIME: 2 hours 50 minutes
SERVES 4–6

500 g (1 lb) gravy beef, cut into large pieces
500 g (1 lb) fresh beetroot
1 onion, finely chopped
1 carrot, cut into short strips
1 parsnip, cut into short strips
1 cup (75 g/2½ oz) finely shredded cabbage
sour cream and chopped chives, to serve

1 Put the beef in a large, heavy-based pan with 4 cups (1 litre) of water and bring slowly to the boil. Reduce the heat, cover and simmer for 1 hour. Skim the surface as required.

2 Cut the stems from the beetroot, wash well and place in a large, heavy-based pan with 4 cups (1 litre) of water. Bring to the boil, reduce the heat and simmer for 40 minutes, or until tender. Drain, reserving 1 cup (250 ml/8 fl oz) of the liquid. Cool, then peel and grate the beetroot.

3 Remove the meat from the stock, cool and dice. Skim any fat from the surface of the stock. Return the meat to the stock and add the onion, carrot, parsnip, beetroot and reserved liquid. Bring to the boil, reduce the heat, cover and simmer for 45 minutes.

4 Add the cabbage, stir and simmer for a further 15 minutes. Season to taste. Serve topped with the sour cream and chives.

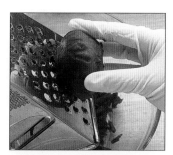

To avoid stains, wear rubber gloves to grate the beetroot.

Allow the meat to cool, then cut into dice using a sharp knife.

Pour reserved beetroot liquid into the soup and bring to the boil.

Chicken and Vegetable Soup

PREPARATION TIME: 1 hour + refrigeration
TOTAL COOKING TIME: 1 hour 25 minutes
SERVES 6–8

1.5 kg (2½ lb) chicken
2 carrots, roughly chopped
2 sticks celery, roughly chopped
1 onion, quartered
4 parsley sprigs
2 bay leaves
4 black peppercorns
50 g (1¾ oz) butter
2 tablespoons plain flour

2 potatoes, chopped
250 g (8 oz) butternut pumpkin, chopped into bite-sized
   pieces
2 carrots, extra, cut into matchsticks
1 leek, cut into matchsticks
3 sticks celery, extra, cut into matchsticks
100 g (3½ oz) green beans, cut into short lengths or baby
   green beans, halved
200 g (6½ oz) broccoli, cut into small florets
100 g (3½ oz) sugar snap peas, trimmed
50 g (1¾ oz) English spinach leaves, shredded
½ cup (125 ml/4 fl oz) cream
¼ cup (15 g/½ oz) chopped parsley

Cut the extra celery into short lengths, then into matchsticks.

Using a knife, trim tops from peas, pulling down to remove string.

Add the parsley sprigs and bay leaves to the pan.

1 To make the chicken stock, place the chicken in a large pan with the carrot, celery, onion, parsley, bay leaves, 2 teaspoons of salt and the peppercorns. Add 3 litres of water. Bring to the boil, reduce the heat and simmer for 1 hour, skimming the surface as required. Allow to cool for at least 30 minutes.Strain and reserve the liquid.

2 Remove the chicken and allow to cool enough to handle. Discard the skin, then cut or pull the flesh from the bones and shred into small pieces. Set the chicken meat aside.

3 Heat the butter in a large pan over medium heat and, when foaming, add the flour. Cook, stirring, for 1 minute. Remove from the heat and gradually stir in the stock. Return to the heat and bring to the boil, stirring continuously. Add the potato, pumpkin and extra carrot and simmer for 7 minutes. Add the leek, extra celery and beans and simmer for a further 5 minutes. Finally, add the broccoli and sugar snap peas and cook for a further 3 minutes.

4 Just before serving, add the chicken meat, spinach, cream and chopped parsley. Reheat gently but do not allow the soup to boil. Keep stirring until the spinach has wilted. Season to taste with plenty of salt and freshly ground black pepper. Serve immediately.

Remove the skin from the chicken, then shred the meat.

Add the potato, pumpkin and extra carrot to the boiling soup.

Pour in cream and stir until the spinach has wilted. Reheat gently.

Hearty Minestrone

PREPARATION TIME: 30 minutes
TOTAL COOKING TIME: 1 hour 25 minutes
SERVES 6–8

2 tablespoons olive oil
2 onions, chopped
2 rashers bacon, chopped
1 potato, chopped into large cubes
280 g (9 oz) sweet potato, chopped into large cubes
3 carrots, sliced
250 g (8 oz) pumpkin, cubed
400 g (13 oz) cabbage, shredded
280 g (9 oz) yellow squash, sliced
220 g (7 oz) green beans, chopped
2 x 400 g (13 oz) can chopped tomatoes
6 cups (1.5 litres) chicken stock
1 teaspoon dried Italian herbs
1 teaspoon dried oregano
⅓ cup (80 g/2¾ oz) macaroni
300 g (10 oz) can butter beans
grated Parmesan, to serve

1 Heat the oil and cook the onion and bacon for 3–4 minutes over moderate heat, or until the onion is just brown. Reduce the heat slightly and add the potato and sweet potato. Stir and cook for 1–2 minutes. Add the carrot and pumpkin and cook for a further 1–2 minutes, stirring continuously.

2 Add the cabbage, squash, green beans, tomato, stock and herbs. Increase the heat and bring to the boil. Reduce the heat and simmer gently, cover, for 1 hour.

3 Add the macaroni and butter beans and cook for a further 10–12 minutes, or until the pasta is tender. Season to taste. Serve with Parmesan.

Slice the squash, chop the green beans and shred the cabbage.

Cook the onion and back until the onion is just brown.

Add the macaroni to the soup and cook until tender.

77

Stir-ins

QUICK AND EASY TO MAKE, THESE VEGETARIAN STIR-INS ARE A FABULOUS WAY TO DRESS UP YOUR SOUPS. SERVE THEM ON THE TABLE FOR DINERS TO HELP THEMSELVES, OR ADD A GENEROUS DOLLOP TO EACH BOWL WHEN YOU'RE DISHING UP. EITHER WAY, THEY TURN A SIMPLE BOWL OF SOUP INTO SOMETHING QUITE SPECIAL.

ROUILLE

Cut 1 large red capsicum in half and remove the seeds and white membrane. Place skin-side-up under a preheated hot grill. Cook for 5 minutes, or until the skin has charred and blackened. Place in a plastic bag and allow to cool, then peel away the skin. Roughly chop and place in a food processor. Cut 1 potato into cubes. Cook until tender and, while still warm, place in the food processor with 2 chopped cloves garlic and 1 egg yolk. Process until smooth. With the motor running, gradually pour in ½ cup (125 ml/ 4 fl oz) olive oil in a thin stream, until you have a thick mixture. Shown here with Bouillabaisse, but also good with most fish soups. Serves 6.

ROCKET AND SUN-DRIED TOMATO PESTO

Add 2 cups (70 g/2½ oz) finely shredded rocket leaves to a food processor. Add 2 crushed cloves garlic and ½ cup (50 g/ 1¾ oz) finely grated Parmesan. Finely chop ¼ cup (35 g/1¼ oz) sun-dried tomatoes and add to the rocket. Process until finely chopped. Add ¼ cup (60 ml/2 fl oz) olive oil and process again until well combined. Shown here with Roasted tomato soup, but good with most vegetable soups. Serves 6.

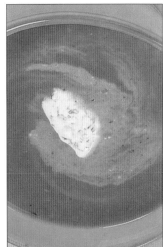

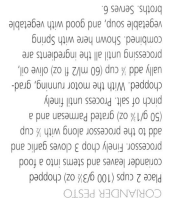

CORIANDER PESTO

Place 2 cups (100 g/3½ oz) chopped coriander leaves and stems into a food processor. Finely chop 3 cloves garlic and add to the processor along with ⅔ cup (50 g/1¾ oz) grated Parmesan and a pinch of salt. Process until finely chopped. With the motor running, gradually add ¼ cup (60 ml/2 fl oz) olive oil, processing until all the ingredients are combined. Shown here with Spring vegetable soup, and good with vegetable soup. Serves 6.

YOGHURT AND HERB STIR-IN

Combine ¾ cup (185 g/6 oz) thick natural yoghurt with 2 cloves crushed garlic, 3 tablespoons finely chopped mint and 2 tablespoons finely chopped coriander. Stir through 1 tablespoon lemon juice and season well. Add a generous spoonful to Borscht, Mulligatawny or Roast pumpkin soup, as shown here. Serves 6.

AIOLI

Crush 6-8 cloves of garlic and place in a food processor. Add 2 egg yolks and a pinch of salt and process until well combined. With the motor running, very slowly add 1 cup (250ml/8 fl oz) olive oil, in a thin stream. Shown here with Spicy tomato soup.

All our recipes are thoroughly tested in a specially developed test kitchen. Standard metric measuring cups and spoons are used in the development of our recipes. All cup and spoon measurements are level. We have used 60 g (2¼ oz/Grade 3) eggs in all recipes. Sizes of cans vary from manufacturer to manufacturer and between countries – use the can size closest to the one suggested in the recipe.

CONVERSION GUIDE

1 cup = 250 ml (9 fl oz)

1 teaspoon = 5 ml

1 Australian tablespoon = 20 ml (4 teaspoons)

1 UK/US tablespoon = 15 ml (3 teaspoons)

Where temperature ranges are indicated, the lower figure applies to gas ovens, the higher to electric ovens. This allows for the fact that the flame in gas ovens generates a drier heat, which effectively cooks food faster than the moister heat of an electric oven, even if the temperature setting is the same.

DRY MEASURES	LIQUID MEASURES	LINEAR MEASURES
30 g = 1 oz	30 ml = 1 fl oz	6 mm = ¼ inch
250 g = 9 oz	125 ml = 4 fl oz	1 cm = ½ inch
500 g = 1 lb 2 oz	250 ml = 9 fl oz	2.5 cm = 1 inch

	°C	°F	GAS MARK
Very slow	120	250	½
Slow	150	300	2
Mod slow	160	325	3
Moderate	180	350	4
Mod hot	190(g)–210(e)	375–425	5
Hot	200(g)–240(e)	400–475	6
Very hot	230(g)–260(e)	450–525	8

CUP CONVERSIONS – DRY INGREDIENTS

1 cup almonds, slivered whole = 125 g (4½ oz)

1 cup cheese, lightly packed processed cheddar = 155 g (5½ oz)

1 cup wheat flour = 125 g (4½ oz)

1 cup wholemeal flour = 140 g (5 oz)

1 cup minced (ground) meat = 250 g (9 oz)

1 cup pasta shapes = 125 g (4½ oz)

1 cup raisins = 170 g (6 oz)

1 cup rice, short grain, raw = 200 g (7 oz)

1 cup sesame seeds = 160 g (6 oz)

1 cup split peas = 250 g (9 oz)

(g) = gas (e) = electric

Note: For fan-forced ovens, check your appliance manual, but as a general rule, set the oven temperature to 20°C lower than the temperature indicated in the recipe.

INTERNATIONAL GLOSSARY

capsicum	sweet bell pepper	cornflour	cornstarch
chick pea	garbanzo bean	eggplant	aubergine
chilli	chile, chili pepper	spring onion	scallion
		zucchini	courgette

First published in 2004 by Murdoch Books Pty Limited.

Erico House, 6th Floor North, 93-99 Upper Richmond Road, Putney, London, SW15 2TG, United Kingdom.

This edition published in 2006 for Index Books Ltd, Garrard Way, Kettering, NN16 8TD, United Kingdom.

ISBN 1 74045 950 4

Printed by Sing Cheong Printing Co. Ltd. PRINTED IN CHINA.